Isaiah, Age 5

My mommy has a big heart.

Julia
Age 5

Mommy, I Love You Just Because...

 Zondervan *Gifts*

Grand Rapids, Michigan

A Division of HarperCollins*Publishers*

Mommy, I Love You Just Because . . .

Copyright © 1997 by Mothers of Preschoolers International
ISBN: 0-310-97320-1

We would appreciate hearing from you. Please send your comments to us in care of the address below. And be sure to recommend this product to your friends. Thank you.

📖 ZondervanPublishingHouse
Mail Drop B20
Grand Rapids, Michigan 49530
http://www.zondervan.com

Senior Editor: Joy Marple
Production Editor: Pat Matuszak
Cover Design: Jody Langley
Interior Design: Anne Huizenga

Published in association with the literary agency of Alive Communications, Inc., 1465 Kelly Johnson Blvd., 3320, Colorado Springs, CO 80902

Printed in China

99 98 97 / HK / 2 3

The MOPS Story

MOPS stands for Mothers of Preschoolers, a program designed for mothers with children under school age, and MOPPETS is the children's program of the MOPS group. As a ministry of a local church, MOPS provides a caring, accepting atmosphere for today's mothers of preschoolers. MOPS International is based out of Denver, Colorado, and produces the MomSense *newsletter and a daily* MomSense *radio broadcast. To find out if there is a MOPS group near you, please call 303-733-5353 or 800-929-1287. E-mail: Info@MOPS.org.*

Foreward

Sometimes we wonder if mothering really matters. We love our little ones so much! But are we making a difference in their lives? There's no report card, no performance review and certainly no raise for what we do as mothers. Does mothering matter? Are we doing a good job? How do we know for sure?

MOPPETS workers who provide childcare for meetings of MOPS groups asked the children what made their moms good moms. In this book, you'll discover why children love their moms and probably why yours love you.

Mothering matters. We find out just how much in the little moments. It's something that happens between wiping the kitchen counter and reading a lapbook. Here's the performance review we've been waiting for. "Mommy, I love you just because . . .!"

Elisa Morgan
President, MOPS International

Mommy,

I love you because you give me

hugs and kisses which show

your love for me.

Danielle
Age 4

All the ways of the LORD are loving and faithful.
Psalm 25:10

Mom looking at me with love.

Danielle
Age 4

Mom and me with love
in the middle.

Clayton
Age 5

My Mom is special because she likes flowers & she likes it when I do good things.

Kaitlin
Age 5

"Cuddlin"

Jason
Age 5

Mommy gives me lots of hugs and kisses
and I love giving them back to her.

Kelley
Age 5

Mommy kisses me goodnight.

Nichole
Age 3

My mom
loves
me
rain
or
shine!

Chelsey
Age 4

Mommy,

I love you because
you play with me and spend
time with me.

Emily

Sing a new song; play skillfully, and shout for joy.
Psalm 33:3

I
love it
when we
go for a
walk
in the
park
together.

Mackie
Age 4 $\frac{1}{2}$

Me and Mom play together and go lots of places together.

Jamison
Age 5

My mom
is
taking
me
to the
park.
I love
you
Mom!

Brooke
Age 5

My Mom loves me
because she grows flowers
and shares them with me.

Alexa
Age 4

My mom looks at the clouds with me.

Danielle
Age 5

Mommy,

I love you because you
make me cookies and cook
my favorite meals.

She provides food for her family.
Proverbs 31:15

My mom takes care of me.

Keya
Age 6

My mom loves me because
she gets my breakfast
for me everyday.

Rachel
Age 5

My mommy cooks and dresses me.

Jena
Age 5

My mom
is
special
because
she
makes me
cookies.

Kelly
Age 5

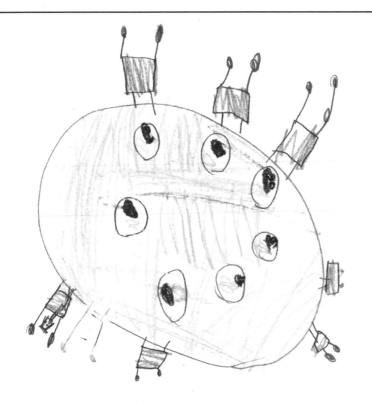

My mom makes the biggest, biggest dinner and the whole family comes and eats with us.

Katie
Age 6

Mommy,

I love you because

you let me do my favorite

things.

The LORD has done great things for us,
and we are filled with joy.
Psalm 126:3

We are
happy
jumping
on the
tramp.

Joshua
Age 5

I love when
my mom plays
Stratego with me.

Austin
Age 5

I like the farm and when she takes me and everyone there. And she lets us ride the pony.

Kyle
Age 6

My Mom is watching me do cartwheels in the grass.

Jenna
Age 6

My mother works in the garden and
plants pretty flowers.

Kayla
Age 5

My mommy loves me because she takes my sister and me to MOPS.

Kraig
Age 5

Mommy,

I love you because

you help me with my chores

and teach me.

Come, my children, listen to me; I will teach you the fear of the LORD.
Psalm 34:11

My mom
makes
a house
for us.

Jennifer
Age 5

I'm thankful my Mom makes my bed for me.

Ashley
Age 6

My mom carries me outside.

Hannah
Age 5

Mommy gives me a bath.

Breanne
Age 4

My mom
takes me to church.

Andrea
Age 5

Mommy,

I love you

just because . . .

Children are a heritage from the LORD, they are a reward from him.
Psalm 127:3

I love my mom because she does nice dances!

Elizabeth
Age 6

Mom and Me dress the same sometimes.

Maggie
Age 5

I love
my Mom
because
she's
pretty!

Rayna
Age 5